APPLE AIRPODS PRO 2
USER GUIDE

Improving Listening Comfort with

Customizable Features

AARON P. BONNER

COPYRIGHT

TABLE OF CONTENTS

INTRODUCTION
Why This Guide Matters

We live in a world where everything is getting smarter —
our phones, our TVs, our homes, even our earbuds. Apple's
AirPods Pro 2 are a perfect example. They're sleek,
intelligent, and packed with features that go far beyond just
"listening to music." But here's the thing: with all that power
packed into something so tiny, it's easy to feel overwhelmed,
under-informed, or just not sure if you're getting your
money's worth.

Whether you're unboxing your very first pair or you've been
using them for a while and feel like you're missing
something, this book is designed to help you understand your
AirPods Pro 2 — in plain English. No tech jargon. No
assuming you're already an Apple genius. Just real talk, real
examples, and real solutions.

This isn't just a product manual. It's a guide created from
one user to another, based on real-life experience and aimed
at helping you enjoy the full potential of one of Apple's most
powerful little devices.

Why I Wrote This Guide

It all started with a moment. I was on a crowded train, trying to drown out the noise with my old earbuds. The person next to me was in full-volume conversation mode, someone's playlist was leaking through weak headphones, and I remember thinking: **"There has to be something better than this."**

A few weeks later, I got the AirPods Pro 2. And let me tell you — it was a game changer. Suddenly, I could cancel out the world, or tap a button and hear everything again with perfect clarity. I was taking calls, listening to music, asking Siri for directions — all without touching my phone. But here's the twist: I realized I wasn't using half of what they could do.

I started digging deeper. I read every forum, watched every video, tested every feature. And the more I discovered, the more I realized how many people were out there *not* getting the full AirPods experience. People spending hundreds of dollars and using just the basics. People frustrated when something went wrong, or too afraid to tweak settings. That's when I knew: this guide needed to exist. Not from a tech reviewer's perspective, but from someone who uses these every day, just like you.

Why the AirPods Pro 2 Deserve a Closer Look

Let's get one thing straight: the AirPods Pro 2 aren't just an upgrade — they're a transformation. Apple didn't just improve sound; they redefined what wireless earbuds could do. With the H2 chip, adaptive noise cancellation, customizable spatial audio, and a charging case that talks back (literally!), these aren't your average earbuds.

They're your personal sound studio. Your pocket assistant. Your hands-free call center. Your gym buddy. Your walking meditation device. And yes, for some, even a certified hearing aid.

But here's the catch: all those features can be intimidating. Not because they're hard to use — but because most people don't even know they exist, or how to activate them.

This guide breaks it all down — not in tech-speak, but in relatable terms. I'm not here to impress you with specs; I'm here to help you use your AirPods in real life: on a morning run, during a Zoom call, while parenting, studying, or commuting. Whether you're playing music, taking calls, or just trying to block out the noise around you, the AirPods Pro 2 can do more than you think.

Who This Guide Is For

You don't need to be a tech guru to get the most out of your AirPods Pro 2 — you just need the right guide. This book is for:

Everyday users who want their earbuds to do more than just play music.

New buyers wondering if they set everything up correctly.

Busy professionals who rely on crisp calls, reliable audio, and multitasking on the move.

Students who need distraction-free studying and easy switching between devices.

Fitness lovers who want secure fit, sweat resistance, and killer sound during workouts.

Remote workers juggling Zoom meetings, Spotify playlists, and Siri reminders.

Parents who want to be aware of their surroundings but still enjoy peace and quiet.

Music lovers who want to hear every layer of a track with spatial audio.

Anyone curious about those little tricks and hidden features that make AirPods Pro 2 worth every penny.

In short? This book is for *you* — someone who invested in a premium device and deserves to know how to make it work for your lifestyle.

A Friendly Tone, A Real-World Approach

You'll notice right away — this book doesn't read like a tech manual. That's on purpose.

Because I believe tech should feel friendly, not robotic. I don't want you to feel like you're sitting in a boring classroom. Instead, think of this book like a conversation with a friend — someone who's already gone through the learning curve and is now walking you through it, step-by-step.

Expect helpful tips, real-life examples, and maybe even a few relatable mistakes. I'm not pretending to be perfect — I'm just here to make things easier for you. Whether you're tech-savvy or not, this guide will meet you where you are.

You'll learn how to:

Set up your AirPods Pro 2 the right way (and make them truly *yours*).

Use the noise modes in the right settings (trust me, this is life-changing).

Get better sound, battery life, and comfort with just a few small tweaks.

Solve common problems without frustration.

Find features you didn't even know existed — and actually use them.

The Goal? Less Confusion, More Confidence

If you've ever felt unsure about:

Which mode you're in

Why only one AirPod is working

How to adjust volume without reaching for your phone

Whether you're charging correctly

How to use Siri or spatial audio

…you're not alone. And you're not doing it wrong. The truth is, even seasoned Apple users miss out on features simply because the information isn't user-friendly.

That's what this guide is here to fix. It's all about helping you feel confident — not just about using your AirPods, but about getting full value from them.

You Paid for Premium — So Let's Use It All

Let's be honest: the AirPods Pro 2 aren't cheap. You paid for premium hardware. So why settle for just "good enough"? Why treat them like basic earbuds when they're capable of so much more?

Don't just block out noise — master how to *tune in* when it matters.

Don't just answer calls — control them like a pro.

Don't just listen to music — hear it the way it was meant to be heard.

Don't just carry them around — let them become part of your daily rhythm.

Whether you're using them on a casual stroll or in high-stakes business meetings, these little devices have the power to elevate your life — if you know how to use them properly.

What to Expect in This Guide

Each chapter of this guide will walk you through one part of the AirPods Pro 2 experience — from setup and settings, to sound quality, battery tips, troubleshooting, and even care and cleaning. But this isn't a one-size-fits-all manual. I've designed the content to reflect the way we *actually* use our AirPods in real life.

Expect step-by-step guidance, visuals where needed, easy wins, and deep dives. I'll point out common mistakes, show you workarounds, and even throw in a few personal stories.

By the end of this guide, you'll know:

How to set up and pair your AirPods with any device.

What every control and gesture does — and how to customize it.

The difference between ANC, Transparency, and Adaptive Audio — and when to use them.

How to get longer battery life, better audio, and smoother calls.

What to do when something goes wrong (and how to fix it fast).

How to unlock features that make you say, "Wait — I didn't know they could do that!"

Ready to Unlock the Power of Your AirPods Pro 2?

If you've made it this far, then you're ready to go from casual user to confident pro.

This guide won't just teach you how to use your AirPods — it will help you fall in love with them. The goal isn't just to hear better. It's to live smoother, move easier, and take back control of your audio experience.

So take a breath, open to the next page, and let's get started.

It's time to *really* hear what your AirPods Pro 2 can do.

CHAPTER 1

Unboxing the Future of Sound

When you unbox your **AirPods Pro 2**, it's not just about discovering a set of wireless earbuds — it's about opening the door to a **premium listening experience**. Whether you're an Apple enthusiast or a first-time AirPods user, this new generation of AirPods is designed to change the way you think about audio. From the moment you first hold them, you'll understand why they're not just another set of earbuds, but a complete **sound ecosystem** that's ready to enhance your everyday life.

But before we dive into all the amazing features, let's take a closer look at **what's in the box** and what to expect from the first impressions of your AirPods Pro 2.

What's in the Box: A Complete Package

Apple's packaging has always been a showcase of **minimalist design**, and the AirPods Pro 2 are no exception. Let's break down exactly what you'll find inside the box:

AirPods Pro 2 (2nd Generation) Earbuds

The earbuds themselves are the centerpiece, featuring Apple's iconic **in-ear design**. They come in their sleek white housing with a noticeable **stem** — but this time, there are a few upgrades to the overall look and feel.

Charging Case with USB-C and Built-in Speaker

The charging case has undergone a major design update. Along with the **USB-C charging port** (a significant improvement over the previous lightning port), you also get a built-in **speaker**. The speaker is used for features like **Find My** and alerts you when the battery is low or when you need to charge your AirPods.

Three Pairs of Silicone Ear Tips (Small, Medium, Large)

Apple includes three different sizes of silicone ear tips for a customizable fit. These tips are an essential part of the AirPods Pro 2 experience, allowing for an optimal **sound seal** and comfortable listening.

USB-C to Lightning Cable

For charging the case, Apple includes a **USB-C to Lightning cable**, but in the AirPods Pro 2 case, you can also charge via the **USB-C port**, which makes charging much easier with the growing adoption of USB-C across Apple devices.

Documentation

As usual, Apple includes a small packet with **Quick Start Guides**, **warranty information**, and safety instructions. This packet is usually minimal, but it's enough to guide you through initial setup and troubleshooting.

The Look, Feel, and Design: Ergonomics, Comfort, and Style

When you first take the AirPods Pro 2 out of the box, it's impossible not to notice the sleek, premium design. Apple has always set the standard for both aesthetic appeal and functionality, and the AirPods Pro 2 are no different. Here's what makes them stand out:

1. Lightweight Comfort

Weighing in at just 5.3 grams per earbud, the AirPods Pro 2 are incredibly light. This makes them ideal for extended use — you'll barely notice you're wearing them, whether you're listening for hours or just having a quick conversation.

The **ergonomic design** ensures that they sit comfortably in your ear, creating a secure fit without causing discomfort. Apple's design philosophy of **minimalism** and **functionality** is clear — these earbuds are **light and unobtrusive**, but they're built to last and feel like a natural extension of your body.

2. Signature Apple Design

The **stems** on the AirPods Pro 2 are slightly shorter than the previous generation, giving them a more **streamlined look**. This update makes them look even more **futuristic** and less bulky compared to the original AirPods Pro.

The **matte white finish** is consistent with Apple's other devices, making them look elegant and high-end. But the sleek design isn't just about aesthetics; it also contributes to their **aerodynamic fit**, reducing wind noise and improving overall comfort during extended use.

3. Silicone Ear Tips for an Optimal Fit

Apple includes three sizes of **silicone ear tips**: Small, Medium, and Large. These tips are **soft, flexible, and hypoallergenic**, offering a comfortable seal for most ear types.

Getting the right fit isn't just about comfort; it's essential for **sound quality** and **noise cancellation**. A good seal ensures you get the best bass response and maximum noise isolation, while an improper fit can lead to discomfort and subpar sound.

Difference Between 1st and 2nd Gen: What's New?

The AirPods Pro 2 may look similar to the original AirPods Pro at first glance, but a closer look reveals several key differences that dramatically improve both performance and convenience. Let's go over the most notable upgrades and why they matter:

1. H2 Chip for Enhanced Performance

The AirPods Pro 2 are powered by the new **H2 chip**, which delivers a host of benefits:

Improved sound quality with richer bass and more balanced treble.

More powerful noise cancellation, allowing for a better seal and greater reduction of outside noise.

Enhanced efficiency, resulting in **longer battery life** despite the increased functionality.

The H2 chip isn't just about sound quality — it also supports the advanced **Adaptive Audio** features, which allow your AirPods Pro 2 to intelligently switch between **Transparency Mode** and **Noise Cancellation** based on your environment.

2. USB-C Charging Port

One of the most talked-about updates is the switch from the **Lightning port** to a **USB-C charging port**. This change makes the AirPods Pro 2 more compatible with modern devices like the **iPhone 15** and other devices that are now moving to USB-C.

The **USB-C charging port** makes it **easier to charge** your AirPods with a **single cable** for both your AirPods and other USB-C-compatible devices, eliminating the need for multiple cables.

3. Enhanced Active Noise Cancellation (ANC)

Apple has significantly improved the **Active Noise Cancellation** in the AirPods Pro 2. Using the **H2 chip**, the new AirPods can cancel out up to **two times more noise** than the original AirPods Pro.

This improvement is ideal for environments like **airplanes, commutes**, or **loud offices**. The new **Adaptive Transparency** mode can adjust the level of sound coming from the environment, ensuring you're aware of your surroundings while still enjoying the music or podcast.

4. New Case with Built-in Speaker and Find My Support

The AirPods Pro 2 charging case now features a **built-in speaker**, allowing it to make sounds for better **Find My** functionality. If you lose your case, it can **play a sound** to help you locate it.

The case now also supports **Find My** alerts, letting you track your AirPods' **location in real time** if they're ever lost. The addition of the speaker also means you'll get **battery status updates** and other audible cues from the case itself.

5. Improved Sweat and Water Resistance

Both the AirPods Pro 2 earbuds and the charging case are now more resistant to sweat and water, making them perfect for workouts or even **running in the rain**.

The **IPX4 rating** on the earbuds ensures that they can handle moisture and sweat during physical activity without affecting performance.

Picking the Right Ear Tips for Comfort and Sound Seal

Choosing the right ear tips is one of the most important things you can do for both **comfort** and **sound quality**. Apple has designed the AirPods Pro 2 to fit a variety of ear shapes, but getting the best seal is critical.

Here's how to pick the perfect ear tips:

1. Use the Ear Tip Fit Test

Apple includes a built-in **Ear Tip Fit Test** that helps you choose the right ear tip size for optimal sound quality and comfort. To run the test:

Open **Settings > Bluetooth** on your iPhone.

Tap the **"i" icon** next to your AirPods Pro.

Select **Ear Tip Fit Test**.

Follow the on-screen prompts and listen to the test tone.

The test will let you know if the ear tips are providing a **secure fit** or if you need to adjust the size for better sound isolation.

2. Small, Medium, or Large?

The **Medium ear tips** come pre-installed, and they fit most people. But if you feel pressure or discomfort, you may need to try the **Small or Large tips**.

If the fit is too loose, you might lose bass response or experience **sound leakage**.

If the fit is too tight, it could cause **discomfort** or pressure in your ear canal, which might affect the overall sound experience.

3. Benefits of the Right Fit

Comfort: You won't feel like you need to adjust them constantly, making long listening sessions more comfortable.

Sound Isolation: A good seal creates a more immersive listening experience by blocking out external sounds.

Enhanced ANC: The better the seal, the more effective the **Active Noise Cancellation** will be, providing deeper silence and better focus.

Better Audio: The right ear tips also help improve bass performance by creating a more accurate sound seal.

Ready to Take Flight

With everything you now know about the AirPods Pro 2, you're more than ready to **unlock their full potential**. From the impressive **H2 chip** and **USB-C charging case** to the **superior sound quality** and **active noise cancellation**, these earbuds are designed to provide a truly immersive audio experience no matter where you are.

Whether you're using them to tune out distractions, enjoy your favorite music, or take calls during your commute, you can trust that your AirPods Pro 2 will deliver **premium performance** for years to come. And with personalized features like the **Ear Tip Fit Test**, **spatial audio**, and **adaptive noise control**, your AirPods will work for you — always adjusting to your needs.

CHAPTER 2

Getting Started – Setup & Pairing

Setting up your AirPods Pro 2 is more than just pairing a device — it's about unlocking a smooth, integrated, and intelligent audio experience. Whether you're an iPhone loyalist, a Mac user, or even someone outside the Apple ecosystem using Android or Windows, getting your AirPods set up correctly is the foundation for everything else.

The good news? It's easier than ever to pair your AirPods Pro 2, and once you're set up, switching between devices — like from your iPhone to your MacBook — can happen automatically. That's part of the AirPods magic.

Let's walk through how to get started, step-by-step, no matter what device you're using. You don't have to be tech-savvy to do this — just follow along and you'll be ready to roll in minutes.

Pairing AirPods Pro 2 with iPhone or iPad (Step-by-Step)

If you're using an Apple device like an iPhone or iPad, the setup process is effortless. Apple has designed the AirPods

Pro 2 to automatically detect when they're near an iOS or iPadOS device.

Step 1: Make Sure Your iPhone or iPad Is Ready

Ensure Bluetooth is turned on.

Make sure your device is running the latest version of iOS or iPadOS.

You can check this by going to: **Settings > General > Software Update**

Step 2: Open the Case Near Your Device

Hold the AirPods Pro 2 case (with the AirPods inside) near your iPhone or iPad.

Open the lid — keep the earbuds in the case for now.

Step 3: Follow the On-Screen Instructions

A setup animation will appear on your screen.

Tap **Connect**.

You may be asked to press and hold the **button on the back** of the case for a few seconds to finish pairing.

If you haven't already enabled **Hey Siri**, it'll guide you through that setup too.

Once completed, your AirPods Pro 2 will be linked to your Apple ID — not just the device you used to pair them. That means they'll automatically work with other Apple devices signed in with the same Apple ID (more on that later).

Bonus Tip: Check the Battery Life Instantly

After pairing, you'll see a battery status popup showing the charge level of both the AirPods and the case. You can always check this later by opening the case near your iPhone or by adding the **Battery Widget** to your home screen.

Pairing with a MacBook or Mac (Manual Pairing)

If your AirPods aren't automatically showing up on your Mac, or you want to pair them manually with another Apple account, here's how:

Step 1: Open Bluetooth Settings on Your Mac

Click the **Apple menu** (top-left corner) > **System Settings** (or System Preferences on older macOS).

Click **Bluetooth**.

Step 2: Put AirPods in Pairing Mode

Open the case with both AirPods inside.

Press and hold the **button on the back** of the case until the front light starts flashing white. This means they're in pairing mode.

Step 3: Select Your AirPods on Mac

Your AirPods should appear in the list of nearby Bluetooth devices.

Click **Connect**.

Once connected, you'll be able to route audio through your AirPods just like any other output device.

Pairing with Android Phones or Tablets

Yes, you can absolutely use your AirPods Pro 2 with Android — although you'll miss out on some Apple-specific features like **Siri**, **spatial audio customization**, and **automatic switching**. That said, the core experience — high-quality sound, noise cancellation, and great mic quality — still works flawlessly.

Step 1: Open Bluetooth Settings on Android

Go to **Settings > Connections > Bluetooth** (varies slightly by manufacturer).

Make sure Bluetooth is turned on.

Step 2: Put AirPods in Pairing Mode

Open the AirPods case.

Hold the **button on the back** until the LED flashes white.

Step 3: Select AirPods on Your Device

Your AirPods should appear in the list of available Bluetooth devices.

Tap to connect.

You'll hear a tone when the pairing is successful. You can now use your AirPods like regular wireless earbuds on Android.

Tip: Consider downloading a third-party app like "AirBattery" or "MaterialPods" from the Play Store for extra features like battery status display or pop-up animations, similar to iOS.

Pairing with Windows PCs or Laptops

Using your AirPods Pro 2 with Windows is possible, and for basic audio functions, it works quite well. Just like with Android, you won't get the full Apple ecosystem perks, but music, video, and Zoom calls? All good.

Step 1: Open Bluetooth Settings

Go to **Settings > Devices > Bluetooth & other devices**.

Turn on Bluetooth if it's not already on.

Step 2: Put AirPods in Pairing Mode

Open the case, keep the buds inside.

Hold the button on the back until the white light flashes.

Step 3: Connect from Windows

Click **Add Bluetooth or other device > Bluetooth**.

Select your AirPods from the list.

Once connected, you'll be able to use them as your input/output device for music, calls, video conferencing, and more.

Note: You may need to manually switch to "Headset" mode to use the microphone during calls in apps like Skype or Zoom.

How to Rename Your AirPods Pro 2

Renaming your AirPods is a simple step that helps you personalize them — and also makes life easier if you own multiple pairs or share a household with other Apple users.

Step-by-Step Instructions (on iPhone/iPad):

Go to **Settings > Bluetooth**

Tap the **"i" icon** next to your connected AirPods Pro 2

Tap **Name**

Enter a new name (like "Josh's Pods" or "Workout AirPods")

Tap **Done**

Your new name will now show up across all connected devices and in apps like Find My. It's also a quick way to tell whose pair is whose in a family setting.

Customizing the AirPods Experience

Apple lets you tweak the behavior of your AirPods Pro 2 so they fit your lifestyle. Here's how you can make them *truly yours*.

Control Settings (on iPhone/iPad):

Go to **Settings > Bluetooth > [Your AirPods]** and explore:

Noise Control Options: Set one or both stems to switch between Noise Cancellation and Transparency.

Press and Hold Settings: Customize what happens when you hold the stem — toggle noise modes, activate Siri, or nothing at all.

Ear Tip Fit Test: Helps you verify that you're using the correct tip size for each ear.

Automatic Ear Detection: If enabled, your AirPods automatically pause when removed and resume when re-inserted.

Microphone Settings: Set it to auto-switch between earbuds or lock it to one side.

Spatial Audio: Toggle on/off and run the personalization setup.

Switching Between Devices – The Seamless Way

One of the AirPods Pro 2's best features is how easily they move between your Apple devices — but only when they're signed in to the same Apple ID. For example, if you're listening to music on your iPhone and then start watching a movie on your iPad, your AirPods will switch audio sources automatically.

Here's how to make that work smoothly:

Make Sure All Devices Use the Same Apple ID

Your iPhone, iPad, Mac, and even Apple TV should all be signed into the same iCloud account.

Enable Automatic Switching

Go to **Settings > Bluetooth**

Tap the **"i"** icon next to your AirPods

Tap **Connect to This iPhone**

Select **Automatically**

Repeat this step on each of your Apple devices.

Tip: If you prefer to switch manually, choose **When Last Connected to This iPhone** instead.

Manually Switching Between Devices (If Needed)

Sometimes, automatic switching can get confused — especially if you're using multiple devices at the same time. Here's how to switch manually:

On iPhone/iPad: Swipe down to access **Control Center**, long-press the audio box, then tap the **AirPlay icon** and select your AirPods.

On Mac: Click the **volume icon** in the top menu bar and select your AirPods.

On Apple Watch: Scroll up for **Control Center**, tap the **AirPlay icon**, and choose your AirPods.

Common Setup Mistakes and How to Avoid Them

Only one AirPod connecting?

Try reseating both in the case, closing the lid, waiting 10 seconds, then reopening.

Forget the device from Bluetooth settings and re-pair.

Not showing up on Find My?

Make sure you paired the AirPods while signed into iCloud.

Enable Find My in your iCloud settings.

No sound even though connected?

Double-check audio output in Control Center.

Sometimes it's as simple as manually selecting your AirPods again.

Auto-switching getting annoying?

Switch from **"Automatically"** to **"When Last Connected"** under Bluetooth settings.

Setup is Just the Beginning

Now that your AirPods Pro 2 are paired and personalized, you've opened the door to an entirely new audio experience. The initial setup — whether you're on an iPhone or a Windows laptop — is straightforward, but it's the customization and seamless switching that make these earbuds so powerful.

From adjusting noise modes and gestures to connecting across platforms and tailoring the sound to your ears, your AirPods are now more than just earbuds — they're your everyday companion for calls, music, meetings, workouts, and everything in between.

So take a moment to explore the settings, test your ear tip fit, and maybe even rename your AirPods with a personal touch. Because when your gear fits *you* — in name, function, and feel — it's not just tech anymore. It's part of your daily rhythm.

CHAPTER 3

Mastering Touch Controls & Siri Commands

When it comes to wireless earbuds, convenience is everything. Apple understands this better than most, which is why the **AirPods Pro 2** give you full control — no phone fumbling required. With just a touch, a squeeze, or even a swipe, you can pause your music, adjust the volume, take a call, or ask Siri to set a reminder, all while keeping your hands mostly free.

In this chapter, we're going to break down exactly **how to use the touch controls, understand the new volume swipe feature**, and **master Siri commands**. We'll also walk you through **customizing controls** to fit your needs — because your earbuds should work the way *you* do.

Whether you're out for a run, on a busy commute, or relaxing at home, this chapter will help you unlock the full potential of hands-free audio control.

Force Sensor Gestures: The Basics of Tapping and Squeezing

The **force sensor** is that little groove on the flat part of the AirPods stem — it's pressure-sensitive, not touch-sensitive. That means instead of just tapping (like the original AirPods), you actually press or squeeze the stem slightly, which prevents accidental inputs from brushing your hair or adjusting your glasses.

Here's what you can do with it:

Single Press:

Play or pause music

Answer an incoming call

This is probably the most-used gesture. You're listening to a song — a quick press pauses it. Press again, and it resumes. Incoming call? One squeeze and you're connected.

Double Press:

Skip to the next track

Want to jump to the next song? Two quick squeezes, and you're there. Works while streaming music, listening to podcasts, or even watching videos.

Triple Press:

Skip backward or replay the previous track

This is your rewind. It's perfect if you missed a lyric or want to hear something again. Just three quick presses.

Press and Hold:

Switch between noise control modes (ANC, Transparency, Off)

Or activate Siri (if customized)

By default, holding the stem switches between **Active Noise Cancellation** and **Transparency Mode**. But as you'll learn later in this chapter, you can **customize this action** in settings.

During Phone Calls:

Press once to answer

Press again to hang up

Press and hold to decline a call

Pro Tip: You'll feel a faint click when you squeeze — like a small tactile response. It helps confirm the gesture was recognized.

The New Volume Swipe: A Game-Changer

One of the most requested features from AirPods users over the years was a way to **adjust volume without using the phone or asking Siri**. Apple delivered in AirPods Pro 2.

Now, you can simply **swipe up or down** on the stem to increase or decrease volume. It's surprisingly intuitive and responsive.

How to Use It:

Place your thumb on the back of the stem for grip.

Gently swipe **up** on the flat sensor area to increase volume.

Swipe **down** to lower it.

There's even a subtle clicking sound in your ear as feedback, letting you know the volume is adjusting. It's not too sensitive, so you won't accidentally blast your ears by brushing it.

Note: The swipe volume feature is only available on AirPods Pro 2 — not earlier models.

When Is This Most Useful?

During workouts, when your phone is out of reach.

On a walk, when you're listening to music and a loud vehicle passes by.

When you're on a plane or bus and want quick volume control without disturbing others.

It's small, but it makes a huge difference in daily use. No more digging in your pocket or asking Siri just to turn it down a notch.

Using Siri: Your Personal Assistant in Your Ears

Love it or hate it, **Siri** can be incredibly useful when your hands are busy — and with AirPods Pro 2, it's faster and more responsive than ever.

There are two ways to activate Siri:

Voice Activation: "Hey Siri"

Manual Activation: Press and hold the stem (if set in settings)

Let's explore both.

Method 1: "Hey Siri" – Voice Activation

This feature is **always listening** for the wake phrase when your AirPods are in your ears and connected to a compatible Apple device.

Just say: **"Hey Siri" + your command**

Examples:

"Hey Siri, play my workout playlist."

"Hey Siri, turn up the volume."

"Hey Siri, what's the weather like today?"

"Hey Siri, call Mom."

"Hey Siri, read my last message."

Privacy Tip: The always-on "Hey Siri" feature doesn't record anything until it hears those two magic words. All processing happens securely and locally.

Method 2: Press and Hold – Manual Activation

If you prefer not to have Siri listening all the time, you can assign **press-and-hold** to activate Siri.

This is especially helpful:

In noisy environments

If you're concerned about privacy

If "Hey Siri" triggers too often by mistake

You can configure this in **Bluetooth Settings** on your iPhone (we'll get to that shortly).

Best Siri Commands for AirPods Users

Let's go beyond the basics. Here are some **real-world, time-saving Siri commands**:

For Music:

"Hey Siri, skip this song."

"Hey Siri, play something chill."

"Hey Siri, what song is this?"

"Hey Siri, play Apple Music 1."

For Calls & Messages:

"Hey Siri, call Sam on speaker."

"Hey Siri, read my latest text."

"Hey Siri, reply 'I'll be there in 10 minutes.'"

"Hey Siri, send a message to James."

For Control & Navigation:

"Hey Siri, increase the volume."

"Hey Siri, turn off noise cancellation."

"Hey Siri, what's my battery level?"

"Hey Siri, directions to the nearest gas station."

For Reminders & Notes:

"Hey Siri, remind me to take out the trash at 7 PM."

"Hey Siri, create a note: buy groceries."

Once you get used to it, Siri becomes an extension of your device — and your day.

Customizing Controls for Each Earbud

One of the best things about AirPods Pro 2 is the ability to **customize what each AirPod does** when you press and hold the stem.

Let's walk through how to personalize your experience.

Step-by-Step: Customizing Controls on iPhone

Go to **Settings > Bluetooth**

Tap the **"i" icon** next to your AirPods

Scroll to the **Press and Hold AirPods** section

You'll see options for **Left** and **Right** AirPod.

You Can Choose:

Noise Control (switch between ANC, Transparency, Off)

Siri Activation

Off (if you don't want anything assigned)

Example Setup:

Left AirPod: Noise Control toggle

Right AirPod: Activate Siri

This lets you quickly switch modes with one hand, and summon Siri with the other. It's great for commuters, multitaskers, and anyone who wants flexible control.

Bonus Tip: Want to avoid accidental Siri triggers while adjusting your earbuds? Set **Noise Control** on both sides instead.

How to Adjust Volume if You Don't Like Swipe Controls

If the swipe gesture doesn't work for you or you're having trouble with it, don't worry — you can still control volume through:

Siri: "Turn volume down."

Apple Watch: Open Now Playing > Use Digital Crown.

Control Center: Swipe down > Adjust the volume slider.

Volume Buttons on iPhone/iPad: Simple and reliable.

Using Control Center for Fast Customization

Want quick access to AirPods features? **Control Center** is your shortcut hub.

Here's How to Use It:

Swipe down from the top-right (iPhone X and later) or up from the bottom (older models).

Tap and hold the **audio tile** in the top-right corner.

You'll see options to:

Switch output (e.g., from speaker to AirPods)

Turn **Noise Cancellation** or **Transparency** on/off

Adjust volume

This is a lifesaver when you're mid-conversation, mid-song, or mid-run and don't want to dig into full settings.

Common Mistakes & How to Avoid Them

Here are a few things that might trip you up — and how to handle them.

Mistake: Volume swipe not working

Fix: Ensure you're swiping on the **flat part** of the stem and not just tapping.

Mistake: "Hey Siri" not responding

Fix: Make sure "Hey Siri" is enabled in **Settings > Siri & Search**, and that your AirPods are selected as your input device.

Mistake: Controls feel delayed or unresponsive

Fix: Ensure your AirPods firmware is up to date and try resetting them if necessary.

Mistake: Accidentally triggering Siri when adjusting AirPods

Fix: Customize the press-and-hold gesture so only one side activates Siri — or disable it altogether.

Personalizing = Empowerment

What makes AirPods Pro 2 so good isn't just the tech — it's how well they blend into your lifestyle. The ability to **control your audio without touching your phone, adjust noise settings on the fly**, or **ask Siri to do things while your hands are full** makes them feel less like earbuds and more like a smart assistant in your ear.

By learning and customizing these gestures and commands, you're not just using the AirPods — you're making them an extension of yourself.

In Summary: What You Can Do with a Squeeze, Swipe, or a "Hey Siri"

Squeeze once to play/pause or answer a call.

Squeeze twice to skip forward.

Squeeze three times to go back.

Press and hold to activate Siri or change noise settings.

Swipe up/down to adjust volume instantly.

Say "Hey Siri" to do everything from calling a friend to setting a reminder.

And with just a few tweaks in settings, you can tailor every one of those actions to suit your routine, your preferences, and your needs.

Next Steps: Try It Out

Here's your challenge: Go through a day using **only your AirPods** to control your music, manage your calls, and talk to Siri — no touching your phone. It might feel odd at first, but by the end of the day, you'll wonder how you ever lived without it.

Ready to take control — literally? Your AirPods Pro 2 are waiting.

CHAPTER 4

Noise Control – Transparency vs. ANC

One of the standout features of the AirPods Pro 2 is their advanced **Noise Control** technology — giving you the power to either shut out the world or let it back in, instantly. This isn't just a gimmick. Whether you're commuting on a noisy train, working in a busy café, jogging along city streets, or simply trying to concentrate at home, **Noise Control modes** let you create your ideal listening environment in real time.

This chapter explores three powerful tools built into your AirPods Pro 2:

Active Noise Cancellation (ANC)

Transparency Mode

Adaptive Audio

We'll explain what each one does, when to use them, how to switch between them, and how to make your AirPods smarter by letting them choose the best mode automatically. So whether you want complete silence or environmental awareness, you're covered.

What is Active Noise Cancellation?

Active Noise Cancellation (ANC) is a feature that uses **microphones and software algorithms** to detect external noise — like traffic, chatter, or engine sounds — and then plays **anti-noise** to cancel it out before it hits your ears.

How It Works

Your AirPods Pro 2 are equipped with:

Outward-facing microphones that listen to external sounds.

Inward-facing microphones that pick up what's actually reaching your ear.

A super-efficient **H2 chip** that processes this information **in real time**, up to 48,000 times per second.

When ANC is on, the AirPods send out sound waves that are the **exact opposite** of the incoming noise. These opposing sound waves cancel each other out — reducing background noise significantly.

When to Use Active Noise Cancellation

ANC is perfect for moments when you want to **focus, relax, or block out distractions**. For example:

During flights (cancels engine hum)

On public transportation

While working in a noisy office

When studying or reading in a café

During workouts at a gym with loud music

When meditating or trying to sleep on the go

Pro Tip: You don't need to be playing music for ANC to work. You can turn it on just for silence — think of it like wearing digital earplugs.

What ANC Doesn't Cancel

While incredibly effective, ANC works best with **consistent, low-frequency sounds** (like a fan, airplane hum, or distant traffic). Sudden, high-pitched sounds — like someone shouting or a baby crying — may still come through, although at a reduced volume.

What is Transparency Mode?

Transparency Mode is the **opposite of ANC**. Instead of canceling outside noise, it uses the same microphones to **let external sounds in**, making it feel like you're not wearing earbuds at all — while still hearing your audio.

How It Works

When enabled, the AirPods pick up the sound around you using external microphones and play it into your ears in real time, blending it with your music or podcast. The result? You can hear both your media and your environment at the same time.

When to Use Transparency Mode

Transparency Mode is great for situations where you need to stay aware of your surroundings or talk to people without removing your AirPods. For example:

Walking or running outdoors

Waiting for public announcements (airport, subway, etc.)

Ordering food or coffee

Having a quick conversation

Working in a shared space or office

Fun Fact: Apple's Transparency Mode is so natural that some users wear their AirPods with it turned on even when not listening to anything, simply to enhance their awareness.

How It Differs from Just Taking One Out

You might think pulling out one AirPod is the same — but Transparency Mode keeps your earbuds in place and lets you **hear in stereo** while still receiving ambient sound from **both sides**. It's more immersive and balanced.

The Magic of Adaptive Audio (New in AirPods Pro 2)

With the **second generation** of AirPods Pro, Apple introduced **Adaptive Audio**, a new feature that blends **ANC and Transparency Mode** automatically depending on what's going on around you.

What Is Adaptive Audio?

Think of Adaptive Audio as your **smart listening assistant**. It uses onboard sensors and machine learning to adjust noise control settings **dynamically and automatically** — increasing ANC in loud environments and switching to Transparency when it makes sense.

What Does It Do?

Lowers volume or increases ANC when a **truck drives by** or a baby cries nearby.

Softens your music when someone talks to you, so you can **reply without removing your AirPods**.

Enhances environmental sounds **just enough** so you stay aware but still immersed in what you're listening to.

When to Use Adaptive Audio

On the go, when noise levels keep changing

In unpredictable environments (train stations, city sidewalks)

When walking through both quiet and busy areas

In offices or homes with occasional conversations

It's the **perfect mode for multitaskers** — those who want the benefits of ANC but don't want to miss out on real-world audio cues.

How to Enable Adaptive Audio

Open **Settings** on your iPhone.

Tap **Bluetooth > AirPods Pro 2 (i)**.

Under **Noise Control**, choose **Adaptive**.

Or open **Control Center > Long-press Volume bar > Tap Noise Control icon > Select Adaptive**.

Note: Adaptive Audio is only available on iPhones running iOS 17 and later with AirPods Pro 2 (with H2 chip and USB-C).

Switching Between Modes: Manual vs. Automatic

The AirPods Pro 2 give you multiple ways to switch noise control modes — manually, automatically, or through Siri. Let's explore each.

Option 1: Using the Force Sensor

The simplest way to toggle between modes is by **pressing and holding** the **stem** of either AirPod.

By default, this switches between:

Noise Cancellation

Transparency

But if you enable **Adaptive Audio** in settings, it will cycle between:

Noise Cancellation

Transparency

Adaptive

You'll hear a chime to confirm the mode change, and your iPhone screen will briefly display the current mode if it's unlocked.

Option 2: From Control Center

Swipe down from the **top-right corner** of your iPhone (or up from the bottom on older models).

Press and hold the **volume bar** (when AirPods are connected).

Tap the **Noise Control icon** in the bottom-left corner.

Choose between:

Noise Cancellation

Transparency

Off

Adaptive (if supported and enabled)

This method is quick, visual, and great for checking your current mode at a glance.

Option 3: Via Settings

Go to **Settings > Bluetooth > Your AirPods**.

Tap **Noise Control**.

Choose your preferred default noise mode or assign one to each AirPod's **press and hold gesture**.

You can also turn off **Automatic Ear Detection** here or adjust **Adaptive Transparency**, which we'll cover shortly.

Option 4: Ask Siri

You can also control noise modes using voice commands:

"Hey Siri, turn on noise cancellation."

"Hey Siri, switch to transparency mode."

"Hey Siri, turn off noise control."

This is especially useful if your hands are full, like when driving, cooking, or exercising.

Advanced Settings: Take Full Control

AirPods Pro 2 give you even more fine-tuning options under settings:

Customize Press and Hold

You can assign the **left and right AirPods** different roles:

One can switch noise modes

The other can activate Siri

This is perfect for users who want quick access to both —
for example:

Left Press & Hold: Noise Control

Right Press & Hold: Siri

Turn On/Off Adaptive Transparency

Apple also added **Adaptive Transparency**, a smarter
version of regular Transparency Mode.

It reduces **loud, sudden sounds** — like sirens or
construction noise — **without blocking softer voices or
ambient sounds**.

To enable:

Go to **Settings > AirPods > Adaptive Transparency**

Toggle it on

Now, you'll stay aware of your environment, but without
being startled or overwhelmed by sudden noise spikes.

Real-World Scenarios: Noise Control in Action

Let's bring this to life with some everyday examples.

1. In the Office

ANC helps you concentrate while coworkers chat nearby.

Transparency lets you hear your name when someone calls you.

Adaptive balances both — lowering noise as needed, but lifting it when someone approaches.

2. During a Workout

ANC at the gym blocks the house music so you can focus on your playlist.

Transparency while running outside keeps you aware of cars and cyclists.

Adaptive Audio for trail runs adjusts seamlessly as environments change.

3. Traveling

ANC eliminates engine hum on planes or buses.

Transparency helps when checking in or ordering food.

Adaptive manages transitions from noisy crowds to quiet waiting areas without you lifting a finger.

Tips for Maximizing Noise Control Features

Try all three modes in different settings to get a feel for what works best for you.

Use the Ear Tip Fit Test to ensure the best seal for effective noise cancellation.

Keep your AirPods firmware updated — Apple continuously improves features with software.

Pair with an Apple Watch for quicker mode switching and volume control on your wrist.

Enable Spatial Audio + Head Tracking for even deeper immersion (more on that in a later chapter).

Your Personalized Sound Bubble

Noise control on the AirPods Pro 2 isn't just about canceling noise — it's about **control**. With three versatile modes — **ANC**, **Transparency**, and **Adaptive Audio** — you're no longer a passive listener. You get to decide exactly how much of the world you let in.

Whether you're lost in a podcast, chatting with a barista, focusing at work, or crossing a busy street, the right noise control mode makes every interaction smarter, safer, and more enjoyable.

Once you understand when and how to use each mode — and how to switch between them — your AirPods Pro 2 become more than just headphones. They become a **real-time sound filter**, perfectly tuned to your life.

CHAPTER 5

The Sound Experience – Spatial Audio & Personalization

One of the most exciting — and sometimes overlooked — features of the **AirPods Pro 2** is how it completely redefines the listening experience. These aren't just earbuds; they're a personalized, three-dimensional sound system that lives in your ears. Thanks to features like **Spatial Audio**, **Personalized Listening Profiles**, **Dynamic Head Tracking**, and **Adaptive EQ**, you get a sound experience that feels immersive, balanced, and designed just for you.

Whether you're listening to your favorite artist, catching up on a podcast, joining a FaceTime call, or watching the latest blockbuster on your iPhone or iPad, the **sound follows you**, adapts to your environment, and adjusts to your ears.

In this chapter, we'll explore:

What **Spatial Audio** is and how it changes music, calls, and movies

How to **personalize Spatial Audio** using your iPhone's TrueDepth camera

How **head tracking** works and when it makes a difference

Additional enhancements like **Conversation Boost**, **Hearing Accommodations**, and **EQ tweaks**

Let's dive into the world of smart, immersive sound.

What Is Spatial Audio?

At its core, **Spatial Audio** is a 3D audio technology designed to replicate the way sound moves in real life. Apple uses advanced algorithms to place sound in a virtual space around your head — so instead of hearing music or voices just in your ears, it feels like they're coming **from the space around you**.

Imagine sitting in a theater. The music surrounds you, a voice comes from the stage in front of you, and footsteps echo from behind. That's the feeling Spatial Audio creates — even with tiny earbuds.

How It Works

The AirPods Pro 2 are powered by the H2 chip, which works alongside your Apple device to:

Analyze the position of your **head** and **device**

Adjust the **audio channels** in real time

Deliver **directional sound** to each ear independently

Combined with **dynamic head tracking**, the effect is stunning — the sound actually **stays in place** even as you move your head or turn your device.

Where It Really Shines: Music, Movies, and Calls

🎵 Music

When using **Apple Music**, select songs (especially in the Dolby Atmos catalog) are mixed in Spatial Audio. This means you'll hear instruments coming from all directions — vocals might float in front of you, drums behind, and synths off to the side.

It turns your favorite songs into **immersive experiences**, especially with high-quality recordings. Close your eyes, and it feels like the band is in the room with you.

Note: Look for the **Dolby Atmos** tag in Apple Music to find Spatial Audio-supported songs.

Movies and TV Shows

Watching a movie on your iPhone or iPad? Spatial Audio makes it feel like you're in a **miniature surround sound theater**.

Explosions rumble from a distance.

Voices stay anchored to the screen.

Rain sounds like it's falling *around* you.

If the movie supports Dolby Atmos or 5.1 surround sound, you're in for a treat — especially with head tracking turned on.

Works with: Apple TV+, Netflix, Disney+, HBO Max, and more (as long as they support Atmos).

Calls and FaceTime

You wouldn't expect Spatial Audio to make a difference in calls — but it does.

With **Group FaceTime**, each person's voice is placed in a different spatial position. It makes conversations feel more natural and reduces "talking over each other" moments because your brain can separate voices more easily.

It's like sitting at a virtual dinner table, not shouting into a digital void.

How to Turn on Spatial Audio

Spatial Audio usually turns on by default when you're using compatible content and devices, but here's how to make sure it's working:

On iPhone or iPad:

Connect your AirPods Pro 2.

Go to **Settings > Bluetooth > Tap "i" next to AirPods**.

Tap **Spatial Audio** and turn it on.

You can also access it from **Control Center**:

Press and hold the **Volume slider**.

Tap **Spatial Audio** and select:

Off

Fixed – keeps the effect static regardless of head movement.

Head Tracked – sound stays in place as you move your head.

Personalizing Spatial Audio Using Your iPhone's Camera

Everyone's ears and head shape are different — and Apple knows that. That's why AirPods Pro 2 lets you **customize Spatial Audio** using a scan of your head and ears.

This feature uses your iPhone's **TrueDepth front camera** to measure:

Your ear geometry

Your head size

The way sound bounces around your face

Then it builds a **custom sound profile** just for you.

How to Set It Up:

Connect AirPods to your iPhone.

Go to **Settings > [Your AirPods] > Personalized Spatial Audio**.

Tap **Set Up Personalized Spatial Audio**.

Follow the on-screen instructions:

Hold the phone at arm's length.

Slowly turn your head side-to-side as the camera scans your ears and face.

It takes less than a minute and runs entirely on your device — Apple doesn't store your scan.

Pro Tip: Do the scan in good lighting and avoid wearing hats, glasses, or anything that could block your ears.

Why This Matters

With personalized spatial audio enabled, you'll notice:

Better instrument separation in music

Sharper voice clarity in movies and calls

Improved directional accuracy during head tracking

It's like tuning a sound system specifically for your body.

Dynamic Head Tracking: Audio That Moves with You

Dynamic Head Tracking takes Spatial Audio one step further. As you move your head, the sound **stays anchored to your device** — so it feels like you're sitting in front of the music or screen, even if you turn your head.

When It Shines

Watching movies: Dialog feels like it's coming from the screen.

Listening to music: Instruments stay in their "place" instead of moving with you.

FaceTime calls: Voices sound more natural, placed spatially around you.

How to Enable/Disable Head Tracking

Go to **Settings > Accessibility > AirPods > Head-Tracked Spatial Audio**.

Toggle it **On** or **Off**.

Or, from **Control Center**:

Press and hold the **Volume slider**.

Tap **Spatial Audio** and choose between **Fixed** and **Head Tracked**.

Some people prefer Fixed Spatial Audio while walking or working out, to avoid the "floating" sensation.

Equalizer Settings: Make the Music Yours

Unlike some other earbuds, Apple doesn't include a full 10-band equalizer in iOS — but you do get some options for adjusting how your AirPods sound.

EQ Presets in Apple Music:

Open the **Settings app**.

Tap **Music > EQ**.

Choose from presets like:

Bass Booster

Classical

Jazz

Rock

Spoken Word

Vocal Booster

Flat (no EQ)

These presets affect playback in the Apple Music app, not system-wide — but if you're an Apple Music subscriber, they can dramatically change the tone and feel of your audio.

Third-Party EQ Apps

There are also apps in the App Store (like **Boom**, **EQ Player**, or **Bass Booster**) that allow advanced EQ customization. Be sure they're compatible with AirPods and have good reviews.

Conversation Boost & Hearing Enhancements

If you or someone you know has mild hearing challenges, AirPods Pro 2 includes features that **amplify voices** and adjust audio to your hearing preferences.

Conversation Boost

This feature uses the beam-forming microphones to **focus on the voice in front of you**, making it easier to hear someone in a noisy place.

How to Enable:

Go to **Settings** > **Accessibility** > **Audio/Visual** > **Headphone Accommodations**.

Tap **Transparency Mode > Conversation Boost**.

Toggle it **On**.

Perfect for:

Noisy cafés

Family gatherings

Soft-spoken friends

Hearing Accommodations

If you've ever taken a hearing test, Apple now offers a simplified version right on your device. You can run this test and create a **custom audio profile** based on your results.

How to Set It Up:

Go to **Settings** > **Accessibility** > **Audio/Visual** > **Headphone Accommodations**.

Tap **Custom Audio Setup**.

Follow the steps to create your hearing profile.

You can also import results from a professional audiogram stored in the Health app.

Once active, your iPhone will **boost or soften** specific frequencies — not just on music, but during calls and voice playback too.

Making the Most of the Sound Experience

Here's how to get the most out of everything discussed in this chapter:

Keep Firmware Updated

AirPods Pro 2 receive periodic firmware updates with audio improvements. Make sure your iPhone is updated and the AirPods are connected regularly for updates to install automatically.

Use the Right Ear Tips

Proper fit = better seal = better bass and noise control. Run the **Ear Tip Fit Test** to find the right size for each ear.

witch Between Modes Easily

Use **Control Center**, **Siri**, or **Press and Hold** on the stem to toggle between ANC, Transparency, and Adaptive Audio depending on your environment.

Try Personalized Spatial Audio at Home

Sit still and close your eyes while listening to a Dolby Atmos track — you'll feel the instruments positioned around you.

Use Apple Music's Lossless and Atmos Catalog

If you're subscribed to Apple Music, explore the **Spatial Audio playlist collections** curated by Apple — they're a great showcase for this technology.

It's Not Just Listening — It's Experiencing

Sound is one of the most powerful senses we have. It shapes how we feel, how we communicate, and how we understand the world. With AirPods Pro 2, Apple has created a product that doesn't just play sound — it creates **experiences**.

From personalized 3D audio that tracks your movement, to EQ tuning and voice enhancement, the AirPods Pro 2 give you tools to make listening more natural, more immersive, and more **you**.

Once you try Spatial Audio, it's hard to go back to flat sound. Once you experience a voice that sounds like it's across the room instead of inside your head, you'll wonder how earbuds ever worked any other way.

So go ahead — explore those new albums, rewatch your favorite film, call a friend on FaceTime, or just enjoy the silence of a well-balanced soundscape. With the AirPods Pro 2, you're not just hearing. You're feeling it.

CHAPTER 6

AirPods for Everyday Life – Work, Calls & Multitasking

When it comes to modern wireless earbuds, the **AirPods Pro 2** stand out not only for their exceptional audio quality but also for how seamlessly they integrate into your daily life. Whether you're working from home, attending a virtual meeting, running errands, or simply trying to manage your tasks hands-free, your AirPods can quickly become one of your most essential tools.

In this chapter, we're going to explore how the AirPods Pro 2 are designed for **everyday multitasking**. These earbuds aren't just for listening to music — they are built to enhance your **productivity**, **communication**, and **organization** across various aspects of your life. From **calls and meetings** to **dictation and reminders**, your AirPods Pro 2 are there to make life easier, more efficient, and more enjoyable.

Let's dive into the key areas where the AirPods Pro 2 truly shine in your daily routine:

Microphone quality during calls and meetings

Seamless switching from music to calls

Using AirPods during **Zoom/Teams meetings** for a professional audio experience

Leveraging **Siri** for dictation, reading texts aloud, and managing reminders

Microphone Quality During Calls

Whether you're in a **Zoom meeting**, having a **work call**, or catching up with a friend, the quality of your microphone can make or break the conversation. The **AirPods Pro 2** are designed to deliver **crystal-clear voice quality**, ensuring that others hear you clearly even in noisy environments.

The Advanced Microphone System

One of the standout features of the **AirPods Pro 2** is the **beamforming microphone array**. This system utilizes multiple microphones to capture your voice with incredible accuracy while rejecting background noise. This technology is designed to focus on your voice rather than the surrounding environment, allowing for a more **natural and clear conversation**.

Dual beamforming microphones: Positioned on the outer part of each AirPod, these mics isolate your voice from ambient noise.

Inward-facing microphone: This mic listens to the internal sound in your ear and helps refine the voice capture, enhancing clarity and reducing echo during calls.

Adaptive algorithms: The AirPods Pro 2's H2 chip processes sound and makes adjustments to ensure you're heard loud and clear, whether you're in a quiet office or a noisy cafe.

Noise Reduction for Your Voice

One of the challenges of making calls in busy environments is the **background noise** — traffic, chatter, or wind can often make your voice sound muffled or distant. The AirPods Pro 2's **active noise cancellation** (ANC) technology isn't just for music; it helps **reduce environmental noise** that could otherwise interfere with your microphone's performance.

Here's what that means for your calls:

Enhanced focus on your voice: The mics are better equipped to pick up your speech while blocking out irrelevant sounds like wind, cars, or loud conversations.

73

Clearer voice transmission: Even in loud environments, your voice will come through clearly, making calls sound more professional and polished.

Seamless Switching from Music to Calls

In a multitasking world, you can't afford to have interruptions that disrupt your workflow. The AirPods Pro 2 excel in **seamless transitions** between tasks, especially when switching between **music** and **calls**.

Automatic Switching

The AirPods Pro 2 are designed to automatically switch between devices connected to your Apple ecosystem. This is especially useful if you are listening to music, and a call comes in — there's no need to fiddle with your phone or press buttons.

Here's how the **auto-switching** feature works:

On iPhone: When you're listening to music or a podcast and a call comes in, the AirPods will automatically switch from audio playback to call mode. The music will fade out, and the ringtone will play in your AirPods.

On Mac: If you're using AirPods with your Mac, and you receive a call on your iPhone, your AirPods will automatically **switch** to the phone call. This means no manual intervention is needed; the system does the switching for you, saving you time and hassle.

Switching back to music: Once the call ends, your AirPods will automatically return to playing your music, podcast, or other media.

How to Control the Switching:

Accepting a Call: Simply tap on the **stem** of one of your AirPods to answer a call. The audio will seamlessly switch to the call.

Ending the Call: A tap on the stem again will end the call, and the music will resume. You don't need to touch your phone to switch between calls and music.

Manual Switching

If you prefer more control over switching:

You can manually switch between **calls** and **music** using the **Bluetooth menu** on your device or through the **Control Center** on your iPhone. You can select which audio source to prioritize based on your current needs.

Using AirPods During Zoom/Teams Meetings

With so many of us now working remotely, virtual meetings have become the norm. Whether you're on **Zoom, Microsoft Teams**, or any other video conferencing platform, the quality of your audio can significantly impact the overall experience. Thankfully, the AirPods Pro 2 are optimized for this exact use case, offering **professional-level audio quality**.

Crystal Clear Audio for Professional Calls

The AirPods Pro 2's **adaptive microphone system** works wonders during virtual meetings. Whether you're attending a client call or participating in a team discussion, the **clear and crisp sound** ensures that your voice is always the focal point, not the background noise.

Active Noise Cancellation (ANC) will block out distracting sounds during meetings, allowing you to focus on the conversation.

The **transparency mode** is ideal for situations where you need to be aware of your surroundings (for example, if you have to hear someone enter the room or be aware of a notification on your phone).

How to Use AirPods in Meetings:

Pairing: Make sure your AirPods are connected to your device via Bluetooth. For Mac users, AirPods will often connect automatically if they're set to your iCloud account.

Audio Settings: For platforms like Zoom or Teams, make sure the audio input and output are set to your **AirPods**. This can typically be adjusted in the platform's **audio settings** under **input** or **output devices**.

Microphone: When you're speaking, the AirPods will use their **adaptive microphone technology** to pick up your voice, while suppressing any background noise.

Real-World Usage:

Imagine you're in a Zoom call with your team, and someone is speaking in the background. With **active noise cancellation** enabled, the AirPods will filter out the distraction, allowing you to hear the conversation clearly. If someone's speaking to you from behind, **Transparency Mode** can automatically adjust to make sure you don't miss anything.

Touch Controls During Meetings:

Pause/Resume: You can pause or resume the call with a simple tap or squeeze on the **stem** of your AirPods.

Mute/Unmute: You can use the **control center** to mute or unmute yourself during a call.

Answer Calls: If you're in a meeting and get an incoming call, you can simply tap to answer without taking your AirPods out.

Dictation, Reading Texts Aloud, or Managing Reminders with Siri

One of the most valuable features of the AirPods Pro 2 is their deep integration with **Siri**. Siri, Apple's virtual assistant, works seamlessly with your AirPods, making it easy to manage tasks hands-free. Whether you're dictating an email, reading messages aloud, or managing your calendar, Siri helps you stay on top of your day without lifting a finger.

Dictating Texts, Emails, and Notes

Let's say you're on the go and need to dictate an email or send a quick text. With Siri and your AirPods Pro 2, this becomes as easy as speaking your mind.

Here's how it works:

Activate Siri: Simply say, "**Hey Siri**" or tap and hold on the stem of your AirPods Pro 2 to activate Siri.

Dictate Your Message: After activating Siri, you can say things like:

"Send a message to [contact name] saying I'll be late."

"Email [name] the report by the end of the day."

"Create a note that says 'Meeting at 3 PM.'"

Review and Send: Siri will confirm your message and ask if you want to send or adjust it. If you're satisfied, just say "Send."

Siri also works with third-party apps, meaning you can dictate messages in apps like WhatsApp or Slack, or dictate longer documents in Google Docs.

Reading Texts Aloud

One of the most useful features of Siri, especially when you're driving or working, is the ability to have your **texts and messages read aloud** through your AirPods. Here's how it works:

When you receive a message, you'll hear Siri announce it through your AirPods.

If the message is from someone you trust, Siri will automatically read it to you, and you can reply with a voice command.

You can also ask Siri to read any other notifications aloud, whether it's a reminder, a new email, or a social media alert.

This hands-free communication is a game changer for those busy, multitasking days where stopping to check your phone isn't an option.

Managing Reminders and Calendar with Siri

Siri also makes it simple to stay organized without touching your phone. You can use your AirPods to manage tasks, set reminders, and schedule meetings just by talking to Siri.

Examples:

"Hey Siri, remind me to call John at 2 PM."

"Hey Siri, add 'finish project report' to my to-do list."

"Hey Siri, what's on my calendar for today?"

You can also set up **alerts**, **alarms**, and **timers** through Siri to ensure you stay on top of important tasks and appointments.

Empowering Your Everyday Routine

The **AirPods Pro 2** aren't just about great sound. They're about empowering you to take control of your daily life through seamless integration, multitasking, and voice control. Whether you're in a **Zoom meeting**, **listening to music**, or simply managing your tasks through **Siri**, your AirPods Pro 2 are designed to enhance every moment without the need to pause and pull out your phone.

As you've seen, the AirPods Pro 2 are much more than just a way to listen to music. With superior microphone quality, intuitive controls, and hands-free access to Siri, they offer a **complete audio solution** for work, communication, and personal organization. So, whether you're on a business call, listening to your favorite podcast, or organizing your schedule, your AirPods are ready to help you **stay productive, efficient, and connected** in every aspect of your life.

Keep exploring, keep multitasking, and let your AirPods Pro 2 work for you — making your life easier, smoother, and always on the go.

CHAPTER 7
Battery Life & Smart Charging Tips

The AirPods Pro 2 are built for performance — but even the smartest earbuds in the world are only as good as their battery. Whether you're listening to music, taking work calls, or using noise cancellation during travel, battery life matters. Apple has significantly improved both the efficiency and flexibility of how you power up the AirPods Pro 2, giving you multiple options to keep them charged, protected, and ready to go.

In this chapter, we'll cover everything you need to know about managing your battery like a pro:

How long the AirPods and case last (with or without ANC)

Charging methods: USB-C, MagSafe, and wireless Qi pads

How to check your battery at a glance (via widgets, Control Center, or Siri)

How to use **Optimized Battery Charging** to extend battery health

Let's break it all down and show you how to get the most listening time from every single charge.

Battery Life Basics: What You Can Expect

Apple's AirPods Pro 2 come with **upgraded battery life** compared to the first generation — and it's more noticeable in real-world usage than you might expect.

You can get **through an entire workday** with a single charge if you're primarily listening to music.

Commuters and travelers can go several days without charging the case.

Quick recharge between meetings gives you multiple hours of use.

The charging case holds **multiple full charges** for the AirPods. That means even if you fully drain the earbuds during the day, just a few minutes in the case can get you back up and running.

Quick Charge Feature: Minutes Matter

One of the best features of AirPods Pro 2 is how **fast** they charge.

5 minutes in the case = about 1 hour of listening time

A **fully charged case** can **recharge the AirPods 4–5 times**

So even if you're on your way to work and realize your AirPods are dead, just popping them in the case while you brush your teeth or get dressed gives you enough juice to last through your commute.

Charging Options: USB-C, MagSafe & Qi Wireless

Apple understands that users need **flexibility** when it comes to charging — so they've equipped the AirPods Pro 2 with multiple ways to charge the case.

Let's walk through each method.

1. USB-C Charging

Apple made the switch to **USB-C** on the latest AirPods Pro 2 (with USB-C version) to align with modern devices and simplify charging across your gear.

How to Use USB-C:

Plug the included **USB-C to USB-C cable** into the bottom of the charging case.

Connect the other end to:

A USB-C charging brick

Your MacBook, iPad, or other compatible device

A portable battery pack or USB-C hub

Benefits of USB-C Charging:

Fastest charging method available for the AirPods case

Can charge from laptops, power banks, and even Android bricks

No need for a special "Apple-only" charger

Tip: If you have an iPhone 15, the same USB-C cable works for both your phone and your AirPods.

2. MagSafe Wireless Charging

The case supports **MagSafe**, Apple's magnetic wireless charging standard. This means you can:

Use the same charger as your iPhone or Apple Watch

Get a satisfying "click" as the case aligns with the charger

Charge at your desk or bedside without wires

How to Use MagSafe:

Place the case (LED side up) on a **MagSafe-compatible charger**.

Make sure it clicks into place magnetically.

The LED indicator will glow **amber** while charging and **green** when fully charged.

Best For:

Home or office charging setups

Nightstand use

Avoiding cable clutter

3. Qi Wireless Charging

If you don't have a MagSafe charger, no worries — the AirPods Pro 2 case is **also compatible with standard Qi wireless charging pads**.

How to Use Qi Charging:

Place the case on a flat Qi-certified pad (centered).

Wait for the **charging LED to light up**.

That's it — it charges just like your phone.

Reminder: Qi charging is slightly slower than USB-C or MagSafe, but it's a **convenient, no-fuss solution** for overnight or office charging.

How to Check Battery Levels: Multiple Ways to Stay Informed

There are several methods to check how much battery you've got left — whether you're using iPhone, Apple Watch, Siri, or even your Mac.

Let's go over each one.

1. On iPhone (Battery Widget)

One of the most convenient ways to track battery is using the **Battery Widget**.

How to Set It Up:

Long-press your **Home Screen** and tap the "+" button.

Scroll down to **"Batteries"**.

Choose a widget size and tap **"Add Widget"**.

Position it and tap **Done**.

Now, every time your AirPods are connected, you'll see:

Left and right AirPods' battery levels

Charging case battery level

If the case lid is closed, it may only show the earbuds' charge. Open the lid to see all three.

2. Ask Siri

Siri can also give you real-time updates:

"Hey Siri, what's the battery level of my AirPods?"

"Hey Siri, how much charge is left in my AirPods case?"

Siri will respond with a voice readout, great when your hands are full or you're on the go.

3. On MacBook

If your AirPods are paired with your Mac:

Click the **Bluetooth icon** in the top menu bar.

Hover over your **AirPods Pro**.

You'll see charge levels for:

Left AirPod

Right AirPod

Charging Case

Tip: You can also go to **System Settings > Bluetooth** for a more detailed view.

4. On Apple Watch

If you're using your AirPods while connected to your watch:

Swipe up for **Control Center**.

Tap the **AirPlay icon**.

You'll see battery levels for connected audio devices.

Low Battery Alerts

You'll get notifications when your AirPods are running low. These usually appear as pop-ups on your iPhone or iPad.

Battery alerts include:

20% remaining

10% remaining

5% warning before shut-off

At 0%, your AirPods will disconnect and stop working — but don't worry, just **5 minutes in the case** will give you a quick hour's worth of juice.

Optimized Battery Charging: What It Is & Why It Matters

Apple includes an **Optimized Battery Charging** feature that helps preserve your battery's long-term health — and it's one of the smartest things you can enable for daily charging.

How It Works

When this feature is turned on, your AirPods will **learn your charging routine** and delay charging past 80% until you need them.

So if you typically charge overnight:

They'll charge to **80% quickly**

Then wait until right before you usually unplug them to complete the last **20%**

This slows battery aging and keeps the lithium-ion battery inside your case healthier over time.

How to Turn It On/Off

Go to **Settings > [Your AirPods]** on your iPhone.

Scroll down to **Optimized Battery Charging**.

Toggle **On** (recommended) or **Off**.

Recommendation: Keep this on unless you're traveling or in a hurry and need a full charge right away.

Smart Battery Tips for Daily Use

If you want to get the most from your AirPods Pro 2, here are some best practices:

Tip 1: Don't Let Them Fully Die Often

Try not to let your AirPods drain to 0% every day. Lithium-ion batteries last longer when kept **between 20–80%** during regular use.

Tip 2: Use One AirPod at a Time for Extended Use

If you're on a long call or listening casually, use one AirPod at a time (mono audio mode). This **doubles your total usage time** while the other one charges in the case.

Tip 3: Store in the Charging Case

When not in use, always put your AirPods back in the case. This keeps them safe and ensures they're topped off for your next use.

Tip 4: Keep Firmware Updated

Apple sometimes releases firmware updates that improve charging behavior. Updates happen automatically when your AirPods are connected to an Apple device and charging.

Tip 5: Avoid Excess Heat

Don't charge or store your AirPods in hot environments (e.g., in a car during summer). Heat is a major battery killer.

Resetting the Battery Cycle (If Needed)

If your AirPods seem to be draining unusually fast or behaving oddly, a full battery cycle reset can help:

Here's How:

Use the AirPods until they shut off at 0%.

Charge them (and the case) to 100%.

Leave them on the charger for another 30 minutes.

Then use normally.

This can sometimes recalibrate the battery sensors and improve performance.

Battery Tips for Travel

When on the go:

Use a **USB-C power bank** for fast recharging.

Pack a **portable MagSafe charger** for wireless top-offs.

Keep a **charging cable in your bag** for emergencies.

Enable **Low Power Mode** on your iPhone to reduce drain from notifications that use audio.

Stay Powered, Stay Connected

Battery life isn't just about numbers — it's about **freedom**. The AirPods Pro 2 are built to keep up with your life, whether you're in a Zoom meeting, listening to music, commuting, or traveling.

With up to **30 hours of total use**, ultra-fast charging, and smart tools like **Optimized Battery Charging**, you don't have to worry about dead earbuds or missed calls. And with flexible charging options — USB-C, MagSafe, or Qi — powering up is always convenient.

When you understand how to manage battery life, check levels, and charge intelligently, you extend not just your daily listening — but the overall life of your AirPods themselves.

So keep them topped off, stay informed, and let your AirPods Pro 2 power every moment of your day — uninterrupted.

CHAPTER 8

Keeping Them Clean, Safe & Working Smoothly

Let's face it — AirPods Pro 2 aren't cheap. They're a premium audio device packed into a sleek, compact design. And just like any investment, they need a little care to perform at their best over time.

Whether you use your AirPods daily for music, calls, work meetings, or travel, they're exposed to dust, sweat, earwax, pockets, and bags. Without regular maintenance, these tiny tech wonders can quickly lose their shine — and worse, their performance.

This chapter will guide you through:

How to **clean the earbuds and charging case safely**

Best practices for **storing and protecting your AirPods**

Using the **Ear Tip Fit Test** to optimize sound quality and comfort

Checking for **firmware updates** to keep them running smoothly

Let's make sure your AirPods Pro 2 stay fresh, functional, and flawless — every single day.

1. Cleaning the Earbuds & Case (Without Damage)

Proper cleaning is not just about hygiene — it directly impacts sound quality and performance. Dust or debris in the mesh can **muffle audio,** and buildup inside the case can **affect charging contacts.** But cleaning them incorrectly can cause irreversible damage.

Let's walk through **what to clean, how often,** and **how to do it safely.**

What You'll Need:

A soft, **lint-free cloth** (preferably microfiber)

Cotton swabs or a **soft-bristle brush**

70% **isopropyl alcohol** (optional, for disinfecting)

A **dry, soft toothbrush** or interdental brush (for speaker mesh)

A **wooden toothpick** or similar non-metal tool (never use metal)

Warning: Never run AirPods under water. They are **sweat- and splash-resistant,** not waterproof.

How to Clean the Earbuds (AirPods Pro 2):

Step 1: Wipe the Exterior

Use a **dry, lint-free cloth** to gently wipe the surface.

Lightly dampen the cloth with **isopropyl alcohol** if disinfecting.

Avoid the **speaker mesh** when using liquid.

Step 2: Clean the Speaker Mesh

Use a **dry, soft-bristle brush** to gently sweep the mesh openings.

For tough buildup (like earwax), gently pick with a wooden toothpick **around** the edges — never push inside.

You can also use a **dry interdental brush** or baby toothbrush for stubborn grime.

Important: Never insert anything sharp or use compressed air — this can damage the mesh or internal microphones.

How to Clean the Silicone Ear Tips:

Gently pull off the tips from the AirPods.

Rinse **only the silicone tips** under water (no soap).

Use your fingers or a cotton swab to remove debris.

Let them **dry completely** before reattaching (do not use heat).

How to Clean the Charging Case:

Exterior:

Wipe with a **soft, slightly damp cloth**.

Use alcohol wipes to clean the surface — but **don't get moisture inside the ports**.

Interior:

Use a **dry, soft-bristle brush** or a cotton swab to gently clean the inside where the AirPods sit.

Carefully clean the **charging contacts** at the bottom of each AirPod slot — buildup here can block charging.

Never put anything wet inside the case.

USB-C Port:

Use a **dry brush or toothpick** to remove lint or dust.

Avoid sticking metal into the port.

Pro Tip: Regular cleaning (once a week) can **extend the life** of both your earbuds and case by preventing buildup and damage.

2. Best Storage Practices When Not in Use

Just tossing your AirPods into a bag or pocket is a quick way to scratch them, clog the mesh with lint, or drain the battery accidentally. Good storage habits keep them clean, charged, and protected.

Golden Rule: Always Use the Case

The case isn't just for charging — it's also your AirPods' protective home.

Prevents physical damage or scratches

Keeps out dust, lint, and liquid spills

Reduces exposure to sunlight and heat

Conserves battery by putting them in sleep mode

Traveling or Storing in Bags? Use an Extra Layer

Consider investing in:

A **hard-shell AirPods case cover** (adds drop protection)

A **carrying pouch** that holds the case and charging cable

A **lanyard loop** for attaching to your backpack or belt

Apple built a **lanyard loop** into the AirPods Pro 2 case — use it to keep your AirPods secure when you're on the move.

Avoid These Common Mistakes:

Leaving AirPods loose in your pocket

Risk of scratching, lint buildup, and accidental drops.

Storing in hot or humid places

Excess heat **damages the battery** and weakens the case seals.

Avoid keeping them in cars, gym bags, or bathrooms.

Throwing them in with coins, keys, or pens

The case's glossy finish scratches easily.

Sharp objects can damage the speaker mesh or charging port.

How to Store for Long Periods (Weeks or More):

Fully charge the case and AirPods before storage.

Keep them in a **cool, dry place** (away from direct sunlight).

Avoid fully draining the battery before long-term storage.

Note: Batteries left at 0% for extended periods may permanently lose capacity.

3. Using the Ear Tip Fit Test: For Sound & Comfort

A **perfect fit** isn't just about comfort — it determines how well your AirPods:

Stay in place

Block out noise

Deliver full bass and crisp audio

That's why Apple offers the **Ear Tip Fit Test**, a built-in feature to help you pick the right silicone tip for each ear.

How to Access the Fit Test:

Connect AirPods to your iPhone or iPad.

Go to **Settings > Bluetooth**.

Tap the **"i" icon** next to your AirPods.

Tap **"Ear Tip Fit Test"**.

Insert both AirPods and press **Continue**.

Play the test sound — Apple analyzes the seal and provides feedback.

What the Results Mean:

"Good Seal" means the ear tip is ideal for sound isolation and quality.

"Adjust or Try a Different Tip" means the fit is loose or leaking sound.

Try:

Twisting the AirPod slightly forward to improve the seal.

Swapping ear tip sizes — Apple includes **XS, S, M, and L**.

Reminder: Your ears may be slightly different. It's perfectly normal to use **different sizes for each ear**.

Why the Fit Matters:

Better seal = **better bass response**

Tighter fit = **more effective noise cancellation**

Proper position = **less pressure, more comfort**

4. Firmware Updates: Keeping Your AirPods Smart & Smooth

AirPods Pro 2 aren't just earbuds — they're smart devices that receive **firmware updates** to improve sound, performance, and connectivity. These updates happen quietly in the background, but staying on the latest version ensures:

Better battery efficiency

Improved microphone quality

Fixes for bugs or connection issues

Upgraded noise cancellation or audio performance

How Firmware Updates Work:

AirPods update automatically when:

They're in the **charging case**

The case is **charging**

They're near a **connected iPhone, iPad, or Mac**

You're **connected to Wi-Fi**

There's no "Update Now" button — but you can **trigger updates** by meeting the conditions above.

How to Check the Firmware Version:

On iPhone or iPad:

Go to **Settings > Bluetooth**.

Tap the **"i"** next to your AirPods.

Scroll down to **About** section.

Check the **firmware version** (e.g., 6A300 or similar).

You can compare your version to the latest one posted on Apple's AirPods firmware updates page (or check online for version history).

If You Suspect You're Not Getting Updates:

Place the AirPods in their case.

Plug in the charging cable or place on a MagSafe/Qi charger.

Leave near your unlocked iPhone with Bluetooth and Wi-Fi enabled.

Check again after about 30–60 minutes.

Pro Tips for Smooth Performance:

Reset if Things Feel Off

If you're noticing weird behavior (e.g., one AirPod not connecting, distorted audio), try:

Forget the AirPods from Bluetooth settings.

Reset the AirPods:

Press and hold the **button on the back** of the case until the light flashes amber, then white.

Re-pair with your iPhone.

Keep iOS Up to Date

Sometimes, AirPods performance is tied to your iPhone or iPad's operating system. Updating your device ensures compatibility and access to the latest features (like Adaptive Audio, Conversation Boost, etc.).

Treat Them Right, They'll Treat You Better

The AirPods Pro 2 are smart, small, and high-performing — but like anything valuable, they need care. Keeping them clean improves audio clarity and mic performance. Storing them safely prevents physical damage and battery drain. Using the Ear Tip Fit Test optimizes your personal sound experience. And keeping the firmware updated ensures you're always getting the best features Apple has to offer.

Here's your everyday checklist:

Wipe down your AirPods and case weekly.

Rinse ear tips monthly (or as needed).

Use the Ear Tip Fit Test whenever you switch tips.

Store your AirPods in the case, never loose.

Check firmware version every few months.

Keep the case and earbuds charged but never overheated.

By building these small habits into your routine, you'll not only **extend the life of your AirPods**, but you'll also ensure they're **always performing at their peak**, ready to meet you in the moment — whether it's work, play, or anything in between.

CHAPTER 9

Solving Common Problems & Hidden Features

Fixing Common Issues & Unlocking the Full Potential

Apple's AirPods Pro 2 are a cutting-edge device, providing a world of seamless audio experiences, connectivity, and advanced features. But like all tech gadgets, sometimes things don't work as expected, and when they do, it can be frustrating. Fortunately, AirPods are generally reliable, and many common issues are easy to resolve. Moreover, as you become more familiar with your AirPods, you'll uncover hidden features that can elevate your experience.

In this chapter, we'll address common problems you might face and provide you with the solutions to get your AirPods Pro 2 working smoothly again. Plus, we'll explore some **hidden features** you might not know about, but will definitely want to try. By the end of this chapter, you'll have the tools and knowledge to keep your AirPods Pro 2 in top shape and fully unlock their potential.

What to Do When Only One AirPod Connects

One of the most common issues AirPods users face is when **only one AirPod** connects to the device. It's frustrating when you're expecting stereo sound, only to hear audio from one ear. Thankfully, this is usually a simple issue to solve.

1. Check the Battery Levels

The first thing to do is check if both AirPods are charged. Sometimes, if one AirPod's battery is completely drained, only the charged one will connect.

Check battery status: On your iPhone, go to **Settings > Bluetooth**, then find your AirPods in the device list. If one earbud is not connected, the battery status will indicate it is empty.

Solution: Place both AirPods back into the charging case, close the lid, and wait for a few seconds. Open the lid again, and your AirPods should reconnect. If the battery is low in one AirPod, it may need to charge for a while before reconnecting.

2. Check for Debris or Dirt

If one AirPod is not charging correctly or not connecting, debris might be blocking the charging contacts inside the case. Dust, earwax, or lint can accumulate over time and prevent a proper connection.

Solution: Clean both the AirPods and the charging case. Use a **soft-bristle brush** or a **dry microfiber cloth** to wipe the connectors on both the AirPods and the inside of the charging case. Be sure not to let any debris fall into the case's charging ports.

3. Reconnect via Bluetooth

If the issue persists, it might be due to a Bluetooth connection issue. In this case, manually reconnecting can help.

Solution:

Go to **Settings > Bluetooth** on your iPhone.

Tap the **"i" icon** next to your AirPods and tap **Forget This Device**.

Place both AirPods in the case and close the lid.

Open the lid and press the **setup button** on the back of the case until the LED light flashes white.

Your AirPods will re-enter pairing mode, and you can reconnect them to your device.

4. Check for Firmware Updates

Sometimes, issues like this can be caused by outdated firmware.

Solution: Make sure your AirPods Pro 2 firmware is up-to-date. Firmware updates are installed automatically when the AirPods are in their case and near an iPhone. Check the firmware version by going to **Settings > Bluetooth** and tapping the **"i"** next to your AirPods to see the version number.

Resetting AirPods to Factory Settings

If none of the above solutions work, you might need to reset your AirPods Pro 2 to their factory settings. A reset can resolve issues like connectivity problems, persistent static, or unresponsiveness. Resetting your AirPods will **erase all settings** and disconnect them from all paired devices, so it's a good idea to make sure you know your Apple ID and password before proceeding.

How to Reset Your AirPods Pro 2:

Place both **AirPods in the charging case** and close the lid.

Wait for about **30 seconds**, then open the lid.

On the back of the charging case, press and hold the **setup button** (located on the back of the case) for about **15 seconds**.

When the LED indicator light on the front of the case flashes **amber** and then **white**, your AirPods have been reset.

After resetting, open the lid near your iPhone and follow the on-screen prompts to reconnect your AirPods.

When to Reset Your AirPods:

When your AirPods are **not connecting** to devices, even after forgetting and reconnecting them.

If you notice **sound distortion** or other audio-related issues.

If you're **selling or giving away** your AirPods and want to ensure all settings are erased.

Finding Lost AirPods Using the Find My App

There's nothing more frustrating than losing an AirPod, but Apple has made it easier than ever to **track** them down using the **Find My app**. AirPods Pro 2 come equipped with **Find My** integration, making it possible to pinpoint their location (or at least play a sound to help you find them).

How to Use the Find My App to Locate Your AirPods:

Open the **Find My app** on your iPhone, iPad, or Mac.

Tap on the **Devices** tab, where you will see your AirPods listed if they are connected.

If your AirPods are nearby and have battery power, you will see their **last known location** on a map.

Tap on your AirPods' name, and you'll have the option to **Play Sound**. The AirPods will emit a sound, making it easier to locate them.

If your AirPods are out of range, you can still see their last known location on the map and get an idea of where they were last connected.

Can You Find an AirPod If It's Dead?

If your AirPods are **out of battery**, you won't be able to make them play a sound, but you'll still see their **last known location** in the Find My app. When you charge them again, the **location will update**, and you can play the sound to locate them.

Lost AirPods Case:

You can also find a **lost charging case** using the **built-in speaker** on the AirPods Pro 2 case. If you misplaced the case, simply follow the steps in the **Find My** app, and it will emit a sound, helping you find it.

Sharing Audio with Friends or Watching TV with Two Sets of AirPods

If you want to share your music, movie, or podcast experience with a friend, the AirPods Pro 2 support a fantastic feature called **Audio Sharing**. This feature allows you to connect **two pairs of AirPods** (or other compatible Bluetooth headphones) to a single Apple device, so both you and your friend can listen to the same audio simultaneously.

How to Share Audio Between Two Pairs of AirPods:

First, make sure your **AirPods Pro 2** is connected to your device.

Open the **Control Center** by swiping down from the top-right corner of your iPhone (or up from the bottom on older models).

Tap the **Now Playing** widget to expand it.

Tap the **AirPlay icon** (the triangle with circles) in the top-right corner of the widget.

Tap on **Share Audio**.

Bring the second pair of AirPods close to your iPhone. When they appear on the screen, tap on them to connect.

Now both sets of AirPods will play the same audio.

Audio Sharing with Apple TV:

If you want to enjoy a movie or show with a friend but don't want to disturb anyone else, you can connect two pairs of AirPods to **Apple TV** for simultaneous listening.

Ensure both AirPods are connected to your **Apple TV** through Bluetooth.

Once connected, both users will hear the movie audio, and each can control their individual volume.

Great for Shared Experiences:

Watching TV: Whether on an airplane or in the living room, share an immersive experience with two sets of AirPods, especially when traveling or in public spaces.

Listening to Music Together: Instead of passing one AirPod back and forth, enjoy music together, each with their own pair.

Tips for Lag-Free Gaming or Streaming

If you're using your AirPods Pro 2 for **gaming** or **video streaming**, latency (audio delay) can be a concern. While AirPods Pro 2 are designed for low-latency audio, there are still some tips to ensure the **best experience** when gaming or watching video.

1. Use Devices with Bluetooth 5.0 or Higher

Bluetooth technology plays a crucial role in audio latency. AirPods Pro 2 use **Bluetooth 5.3**, which offers faster data transfer and lower latency compared to older Bluetooth versions.

Solution: Ensure you're using a **Bluetooth 5.0+ compatible device** for the best performance. Many newer iPhones, iPads, and Macs support Bluetooth 5.0 or higher.

2. Reduce Background Apps

Background apps can drain resources and introduce audio lag. To optimize your AirPods Pro 2 experience, close any unnecessary apps that might be running in the background.

Solution: On iPhone, swipe up and **close apps** that aren't in use to free up processing power for gaming or streaming.

3. Use Wired Audio for Serious Gaming

While AirPods are great for casual gaming, serious gamers looking for the absolute **lowest latency** might prefer wired headphones. If you're using a gaming console, consider using **wired headphones** for a lag-free experience.

Solution: When gaming on platforms like PlayStation or Xbox, use **Bluetooth adapters** or wired connections if available.

4. Keep Your Devices Close

The closer you are to your connected device, the lower the latency. Keep your iPhone, iPad, or other connected device **within a reasonable distance** (around 10-15 feet) to avoid

Making Your AirPods Pro 2 Work for You

The AirPods Pro 2 are incredibly powerful tools, but like any device, it's important to know how to solve common problems when they arise and unlock hidden features to get the most out of your AirPods. Whether you're dealing with connectivity issues, tracking down a lost AirPod, or enjoying audio sharing with a friend, the solutions and tips we've covered ensure that your AirPods Pro 2 experience is smooth and stress-free.

As you continue to explore the features of your AirPods, remember that they're designed to simplify your life — not complicate it. By keeping your AirPods Pro 2 clean, properly charged, and updated, and by knowing how to troubleshoot common issues, you'll be able to enjoy their full potential at all times.

Stay connected, stay productive, and above all, enjoy your **AirPods Pro 2**. They're here to make every moment sound better.

CONCLUSION

Making the Most of Your AirPods Pro 2

As we reach the end of this guide, you've now unlocked the full potential of your **AirPods Pro 2**. From the unboxing experience to mastering advanced features and troubleshooting, you are now equipped to use your AirPods Pro 2 to their fullest, whether you're using them for work, entertainment, or everything in between.

We've covered a lot of ground throughout this book — from the basics of setup and pairing to customizing your sound experience with **Spatial Audio**. You've learned how to manage your AirPods during calls, meetings, and multitasking scenarios, and you've discovered how to troubleshoot common problems. In essence, you now know how to make your AirPods a natural extension of your everyday life.

But this is just the beginning. Now that you've mastered the fundamentals, the true enjoyment comes from experimenting with features, discovering new ways to integrate them into your routine, and constantly finding new ways your AirPods can enhance your life. Let's take a moment to recap everything you've learned and emphasize how to continue making the most of your AirPods Pro 2.

Recap of What You've Learned

Through this guide, you've become proficient in:

Setting Up and Pairing Your AirPods Pro 2 You've learned how to pair your AirPods Pro 2 with **iPhones**, **iPads**, **Macs**, and even **Android** and **Windows** devices. You're now a pro at navigating through the setup process and managing connections between devices seamlessly.

Mastering Touch Controls & Siri Commands Whether it's controlling music, answering calls, or activating Siri, you now know how to use **force sensor gestures** and make the most of Siri. The ability to customize your controls allows you to tailor your experience to your preferences, making your AirPods Pro 2 not just a listening device, but a fully personalized tool.

Getting the Best Sound Experience with Spatial Audio With **Spatial Audio** and **Personalized Listening Profiles**, you can immerse yourself in sound like never before. Whether it's for music, movies, or gaming, you've learned how to use head-tracking and adjust your sound preferences to fit your unique hearing profile.

Using Your AirPods for Everyday Life
Your AirPods are not just for music — they're a **tool for productivity**. You now know how to seamlessly switch from music to calls, manage meetings through **Zoom/Teams**, and get work done by dictating messages and setting reminders using Siri.

Troubleshooting & Hidden Features
By now, you've encountered and solved common problems, such as when only one AirPod connects or when you need to reset your device. You've also unlocked hidden features like **Audio Sharing** and **Find My** to locate lost AirPods.

All of these features are designed to make your life easier, not more complicated. The AirPods Pro 2 are meant to be an effortless part of your routine, enhancing both your productivity and enjoyment. They are a remarkable piece of technology, but what makes them truly exceptional is their ability to seamlessly integrate into your day-to-day activities.

Exploring More Features and Enjoying Your AirPods Pro 2

Now that you've got a solid understanding of what your AirPods Pro 2 can do, it's time to dive deeper into some of the more subtle, but incredibly powerful, features. The AirPods Pro 2 are capable of **adapting to your environment**, whether you're listening to music in a quiet space, taking a call in a noisy coffee shop, or enjoying a podcast on a walk.

Adaptive Audio: A Game-Changer for Noise Management

The AirPods Pro 2's **Adaptive Audio** is one of those features that might go unnoticed unless you're actively trying to see how it adjusts to your needs. By intelligently switching between **Active Noise Cancellation** and **Transparency Mode**, your AirPods are designed to ensure you get the right level of environmental awareness without sacrificing audio quality. Whether you're in a loud city or a peaceful park, **Adaptive Audio** enhances your listening experience without you having to think about it.

Personalized Spatial Audio

Spatial Audio takes your music and movies to a new level of immersion. But what makes it even more powerful is the ability to **personalize** it based on your specific hearing profile. Using the **iPhone camera**, you can map your ear shape and customize your experience so that each piece of audio — whether it's a song, movie, or call — is tuned specifically for you. This level of personalization is a great example of how technology can be used to cater to your unique needs.

Siri Integration for Hands-Free Productivity

If you haven't fully explored **Siri** yet, now's the time. Siri on AirPods Pro 2 isn't just about playing music or setting reminders — it's about **full hands-free control** of your day. You can **dictate messages**, **create calendar events**, and **manage reminders**, all while keeping your hands free to continue working, driving, or whatever else you're doing.

One of the most practical uses of Siri is its ability to read incoming messages aloud. If you're walking, working, or cooking, Siri can announce your texts, allowing you to stay connected without having to pick up your phone.

Sharing Audio with Friends

Audio Sharing is one of the most fun and social features of the AirPods Pro 2. Whether you're on a long flight or just hanging out with a friend, you can **pair two sets of AirPods**

to a single device to listen to the same music, watch the same movie, or enjoy the same podcast. This feature is a perfect way to connect with others, share experiences, and enjoy media together without needing extra speakers or other devices.

Why Technology Should Make Life Easier, Not Harder

One of the key takeaways from this guide is that **technology is here to make life easier, not harder**. With **AirPods Pro 2**, Apple has provided a device that is designed to seamlessly integrate into your life and simplify your daily activities. Whether you're managing work calls, enjoying music during your workout, or simply using Siri to keep track of reminders, these earbuds enhance your life by staying **intuitive**, **responsive**, and **easy to use**.

Technology has the potential to overwhelm us, especially as new gadgets come with seemingly endless features and settings. But Apple has perfected the art of **streamlining** technology to work for you — not against you. The **AirPods Pro 2** are the epitome of this approach. They don't just sound great; they work **intuitively**, **adapting to your environment** and providing the **flexibility** to cater to your needs.

The ability to manage work, play, and everything in between — all from a pair of wireless earbuds — shows just how powerful the **AirPods Pro 2** can be. From simplifying tasks to enhancing experiences, your AirPods are built to do more than just play music. They can become your **go-to tool for productivity**, **connection**, and entertainment.

A Final Thank You and Invitation to Share Your Story

We've covered a lot in this guide, but ultimately, it's up to you to discover how AirPods Pro 2 can **fit seamlessly** into your own unique lifestyle. Whether you're using them to elevate your professional calls, improve your workout routine, or enjoy music and movies like never before, the key to making the most of your AirPods is to **explore**, **experiment**, and **have fun**.

Thank you for taking the time to read through this guide. I hope you now feel confident and excited about making the most of your AirPods Pro 2. The best part about technology is that it's **constantly evolving** — and as new updates and features roll out, your AirPods will continue to offer more and more ways to simplify your life.

I'd love to hear how you're using your AirPods Pro 2. Whether you've discovered new features, customized them to suit your needs, or simply found them to be an indispensable part of your routine, your **AirPods story** matters.

Share your experiences with others — whether through social media, a review, or just by telling a friend. You never know, your experience might help someone else unlock the full potential of their AirPods Pro 2.

Final Thought: Embrace the Future of Audio

The **AirPods Pro 2** are much more than a pair of wireless earbuds. They are a testament to how technology can **simplify**, **enhance**, and **transform** the way we interact with the world around us. As you continue using your AirPods, take the time to enjoy the incredible sound, explore the features, and experiment with the settings that work best for you.

Remember: it's not about getting the latest tech just for the sake of it. It's about how that technology improves **your life**, **your productivity**, and **your enjoyment**. And with AirPods Pro 2, you've got a device that's ready to do just that.

Thank you for trusting this guide to help you navigate the features, fixes, and hidden gems of the AirPods Pro 2. Now, go ahead — put them to the test, and make the most of your AirPods experience!

www.ingramcontent.com/pod-product-compliance
Lightning Source LLC
LaVergne TN
LVHW051659050326
832903LV00032B/3894